Animals

Les animaux

lay zah-nee-moh

Illustrated by Clare Beaton

Illustré par Clare Beaton

BARRON'S

cat

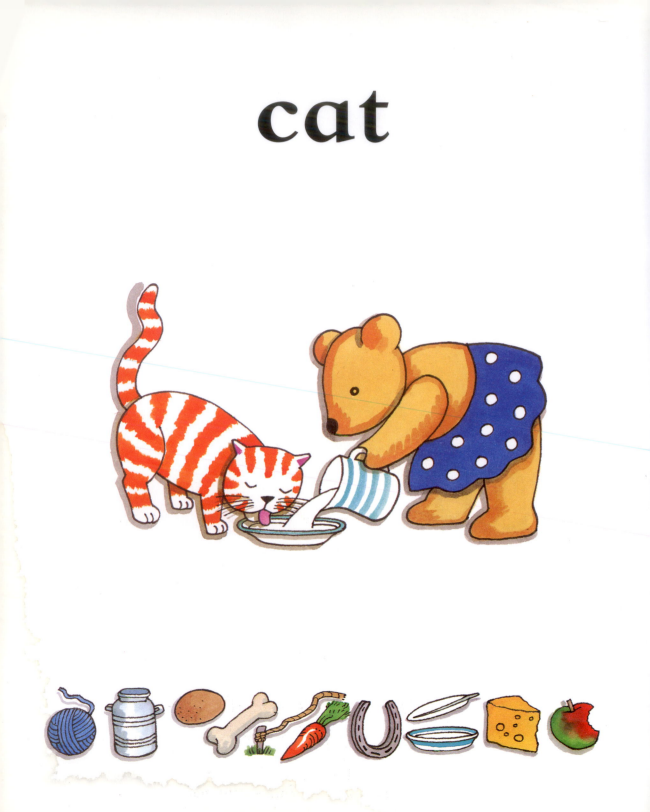

le chat

le sh-ah
(e in le sounds like e in English word the)

dog

le chien

le shee-yah

horse

le cheval

le sh-vahl

COW

la vache

lah vah-sh

rabbit

le lapin

le lah-pah

sheep

le mouton

le moo-toh

goat

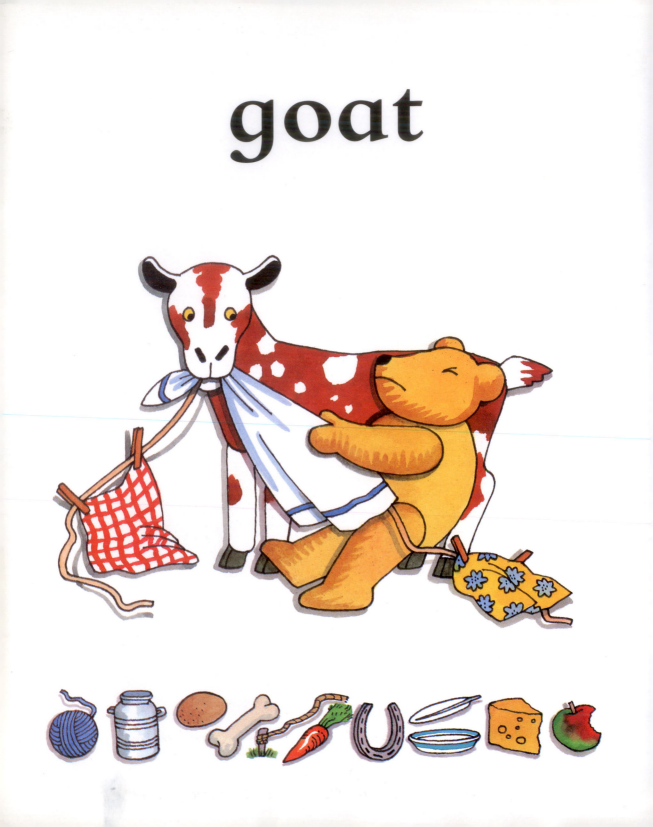

la chèvre

lah sh-eh-vr
(French letter è sounds like eh in English word pet.)

chicken

le poulet

le poo-lay

mouse

la souris

lah soo-ree

pig

le cochon

le koh-sh-oh

duck

le canard

le kan-nahr

A simple guide to pronouncing French words

• Read this guide as naturally as possible, as if it were English.
• Letter e in the French word le sounds like e in the English word the.
• Remember that the final consonants in French generally are silent.

Les animaux	lay zah-nee-moh	**Animals**
le chat	le sh-ah	**cat**
le chien	le shee-yah	**dog**
le cheval	le sh-vahl	**horse**
la vache	lah vah-sh	**cow**
le lapin	le lah-pah	**rabbit**
le mouton	le moo-toh	**sheep**
la chèvre	lah sh-eh-vr	**goat**
le poulet	le poo-lay	**chicken**
la souris	lah soo-ree	**mouse**
le cochon	le koh-sh-oh	**pig**
le canard	le kah-nahr	**duck**